D0264920

EGMONT
We bring stories to life

First published in Great Britain in 2017 by Egmont UK Limited,
The Yellow Building, 1 Nicholas Road, London W11 4AN

© 2017 Disney/Pixar

Written by Chloë Boyes
Designed by Jeannette O'Toole

ISBN 978 1 4052 8761 6
67240/1
Printed in Italy

Materials and characters from the movies *Cars* and *Cars 3*. Copyright © 2017 Disney Enterprises, Inc. and Pixar. All rights reserved.
Disney/Pixar elements © Disney/Pixar; not including underlying vehicles are the property of the following third parties, as applicable: AMC, El Camino, Gremlin, Hudson, Hudson Hornet, Nash Ambassador, Pacer, Plymouth Superbird and Willys are trademarks of FCA US LLC; Dodge®, Jeep® and the Jeep® grille design are registered trademarks of FCA US LLC; IVECO is a trademark of IVECO SpA; Petty marks used by permission of Petty Marketing LLC; Mack is a trademark of Mack Trucks, Inc.; Maserati logos and model designations are trademarks of Maserati S.p.A. and are used under license; Fairlane, Ford Coupe, Mercury, Model T, Mondeo, and Mustang are trademarks of Ford Motor Company; Darrell Waltrip marks used by permission of Darrell Waltrip Motor Sports; Carrera and Porsche are trademarks of Porsche; Sarge's rank insignia design used with the approval of the U.S. Army; Volkswagen trademarks, design patents and copyrights are used with the approval of the owner, Volkswagen AG; Bentley is a trademark of Bentley Motors Limited; BMW, MINI and Cooper are trademarks of BMW AG; FIAT and Topolino are trademarks of FCA Group Marketing S.p.A.; Cadillac Coupe DeVille, Chevrolet, Chevrolet Impala, Corvette, El Dorado, H-1 Hummer, and Monte Carloare trademarks of General Motors; Range Rover and Land Rover are trademarks of Land Rover; © & TM 2012 LTI LTD trading as the London Taxi Company; The trademarks OPEL, VAUXHALL, ASTRA, CORSA, MERIVA and ZAFIRA are registered trademarks of Opel Eisenach GmbH/GM UK Ltd.; Peugeot is a trademark of Peugeot; Tatra is a trademark of TATRA, a.s.; Majesta is a trademark of Toyota; Mario Andretti marks used by permission of Mario Andretti; Mazda Miata is a trademark of Mazda Motor Corporation; Nash Ambassador is a trademark of FCA US LLC.; FIAT is a trademark of FIAT S.p.A.; Dodge is a trademark of Chrysler LLC; Volkswagen trademarks, design patents and copyrights are used with the approval of the owner Volkswagen AG. ; Background inspired by the Cadillac Ranch by Ant Farm (Lord, Michels and Marquez) © 1974.

All rights reserved. No part of this publication may be reproduced, stored in a retrieval system, or transmitted in any form or by any means, electronic, mechanical, photocopying, recording or otherwise, without the prior permission of the publisher and copyright owner.

Parental guidance is advised for all craft and colouring activities. Always ask an adult to help when using glue, paint and scissors.
Wear protective clothing and cover surfaces to avoid staining.

Stay safe online. Any website addresses listed in this book are correct at the time of going to print. However, Egmont is not responsible for content hosted by third parties. Please be aware that online content can be subject to change and websites can contain content that is unsuitable for children. We advise that all children are supervised when using the internet.

This **BOOK** belongs to:

....

....

....

Disney · PIXAR

Cars

ANNUAL 2018

What's INSIDE?

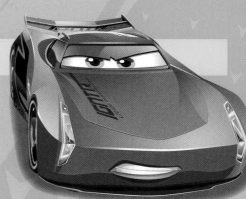

Meet the
CARS

LIGHTNING MCQUEEN

Lightning McQueen, number 95, is the Piston Cup King. But can he keep up with the new generation of speedy racers?

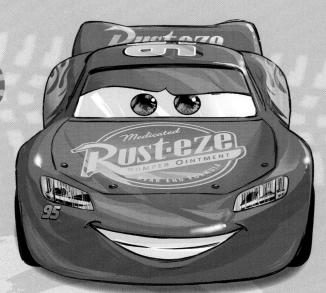

I. Am. **SPEED!**

CRUZ RAMIREZ

A smart, young trainer, ready to push Lightning McQueen to do his best. Can she help him to win one more Piston Cup?

Cruz to **VICTORY!**

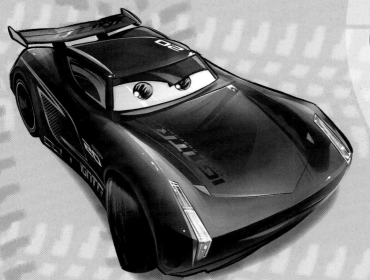

JACKSON STORM

One of the Next Generation of racers. Storm doesn't care about making friends or being a hero — he is only interested in winning.

MACK

Lightning McQueen's driver and his first real friend in the racing world. Hard-working and cheerful, Mack isn't afraid of driving through the night to get Lightning McQueen to races on time.

LUIGI AND GUIDO

Our favourite double act and the core of Lightning McQueen's racing crew. Luigi has a passion for Ferraris and his assistant, Guido, is the fastest forklift in the business.

MISS FRITTER

The formidable demolition derby legend and member of the Thunder Hollow Crazy 8 Crew. Despite her menacing look and trash talking, Miss Fritter has a soft spot for Lightning McQueen.

DOC HUDSON

Lightning McQueen's mentor and crew chief. Although he's no longer around, Doc continues to be a role-model for Lightning and is shown to be a true hero, on and off the track.

LOUISE NASH

The 'First Lady of Racing', Louise won three back-to-back races in her first season and led the way for female racers. Louise is fearless and she still loves kicking off her hubcaps and racing at top speed.

NATALIE CERTAIN

An incredibly smart statistical analyst — Natalie can always work out who will win a race!

SMOKEY

A clever and inventive mechanic, Smokey used to be Doc's best friend and crew chief. Can he help Lightning and Cruz get ready for the new season?

JUNIOR 'MIDNIGHT' MOON

Junior Moon was one of the first stock car racers. Using wooded back roads instead of tracks, this racing legend inspired many of the heroes we know today, including Doc Hudson.

STORY Part 1

Lightning McQueen and his friends are enjoying the racing season. They love competing with each other and playing pranks.

But they have competition. At the Copper Canyon Speedway, a dark, sleek car speeds past Lightning to take first place. This is Jackson Storm and he is from a new generation of racers.

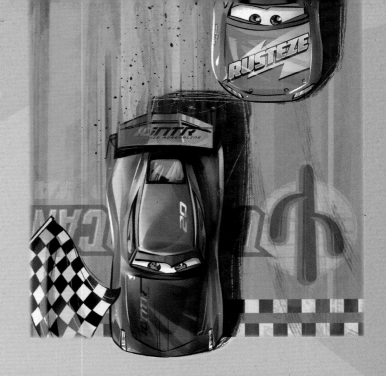

Lightning McQueen heads over to congratulate him when the race is over. 'Nice to finally beat you,' replies Jackson Storm.

Sponsors of the veteran racers start to replace them with Next Gens. Soon, the veterans are replaced or retire, until Lightning is the only one left.

At the Los Angeles International Speedway, the last race of the season begins and Lightning is determined to win. Jackson Storm is in the lead but Lightning pushes on. As Lightning closes the gap he pushes too hard — he skids and loses control. Everything goes dark.

CRAASSH!

THE STORY CONTINUES ON PAGE 18

League of
LEGENDS

Legends, Louise Nash, Smokey and River Scott, raced alongside Doc Hudson. They still love to race for fun.

Can you **TRACE** their tracks without taking your pencil off the page?

STORM
Ahead

Jackson Storm doesn't want to be a hero — he just wants to win. **TRACK** the path he'll need to take through the maze to get to the finish line.

START

FINISH

Check your answer on page 68.

15

Who is your HERO?

The world of racing is changing and Lightning McQueen feels out of place. **JOIN** the dots to show which of his heroes can motivate him to keep going.

RIVER SCOTT

Louise Nash

JUNIOR MOON

Smokey

DRAW
Your Hero

People we admire and look up to can help to make us feel better when things are hard. Use the space to **DRAW** someone who is a hero to you.

HELPFUL

WISE

KIND

SUPPORTIVE

CLEVER

HARDWORKING

BRAVE

COLOUR the flags next to the words that best describe this person.

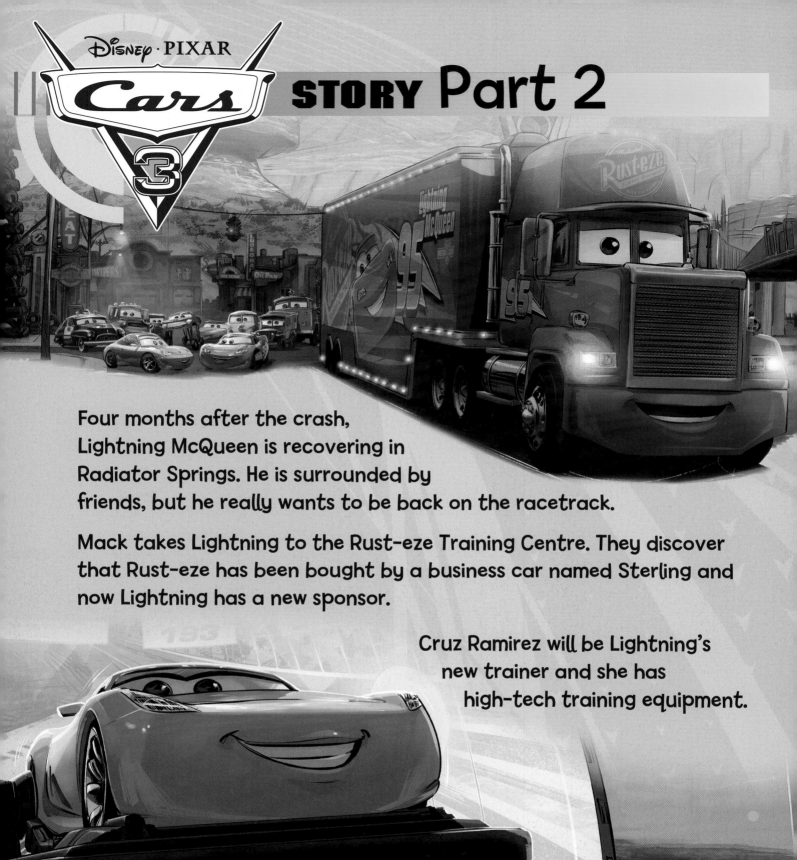

Four months after the crash, Lightning McQueen is recovering in Radiator Springs. He is surrounded by friends, but he really wants to be back on the racetrack.

Mack takes Lightning to the Rust-eze Training Centre. They discover that Rust-eze has been bought by a business car named Sterling and now Lightning has a new sponsor.

Cruz Ramirez will be Lightning's new trainer and she has high-tech training equipment.

Lightning gets a new body wrap and Cruz starts his training. It's tough as Lightning is used to racing outside.

Lightning wants to race on real tracks and asks to go to the beach. Cruz finds this hard as she has only ever raced in the training centre.

Lightning gives Cruz some tips and she starts to get the hang of it.

They leave the beach to find somewhere to get their tyres muddy and find a track at Thunder Hollow Speedway.

But they realise too late that this is a demolition derby!

THE STORY CONTINUES ON PAGE 26

Next GENERATION

Jackson Storm is in the lead again — but something is not quite right. **SPOT** 5 differences between the pictures below.

COLOUR a star when you find a difference.

Check your answers on page 68.

WHERE is Everybody?

Team work is the most important part of racing.

A

B

C

D

E

F

CIRCLE each member of Lightning McQueen's crew you can see in the picture.

Who is missing from the picture?

Check your answers on page 68.

Cruz
RAMIREZ

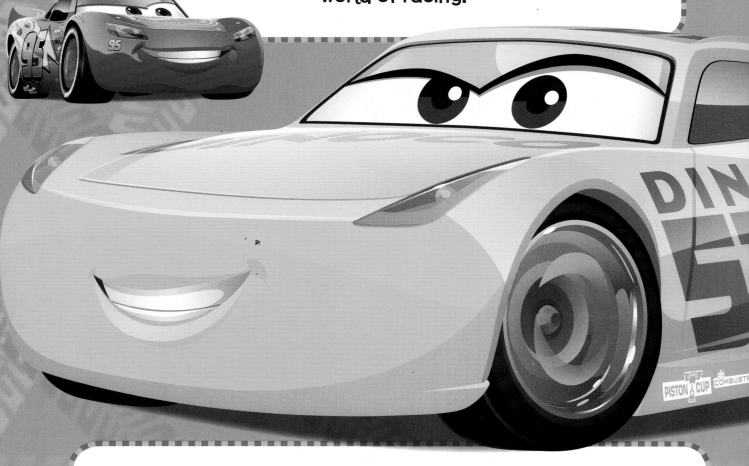

Meet **CRUZ RAMIREZ**, Lightning McQueen's trainer on the new high-tech racing simulator. Her job is to get Lightning race-ready and bring him up to speed with new racing technology. She is smart and tech-savvy, but has a lot to learn about the real world of racing.

Cruz wants to learn as much as she can from Lightning McQueen. Together, they can use Cruz's scientific mind and Lightning's experience to create the best possible racing team!

COLOUR
in Cruz

This picture will help you to choose which colours to use.

Now you've heard all about Cruz, can you **COLOUR** her in?

23

Who is WHO?

Can you **MATCH** the characters to their descriptions and work out who is who?

DRAW lines to match the character.

1

I am new to the racing scene, but I'm already the fastest. Winning is the only thing that matters.

A

B

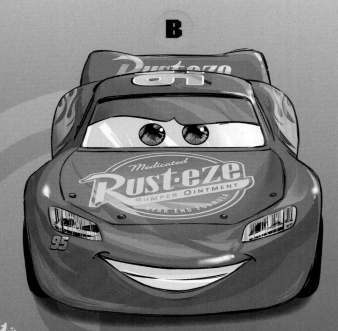

2

I am a young trainer with a love of technology. I have so much to learn about the world of racing but I'm super-keen to get started.

24

3

I am a famous race car. I have competed in many Piston Cup finals and still love to race.

C

D

4

I used to train "The Fabulous Hudson Hornet". Now, I'm helping Lightning and Cruz get ready to race.

5

I am part of the Thunder Hollow Crazy Eight Crew and undefeated demolition derby champion.

E

Check your answers on page 68.

STORY Part 3

Cruz and Lightning are locked inside the track and there is no escape. Demolition derby champion, Miss Fritter, chases after them.

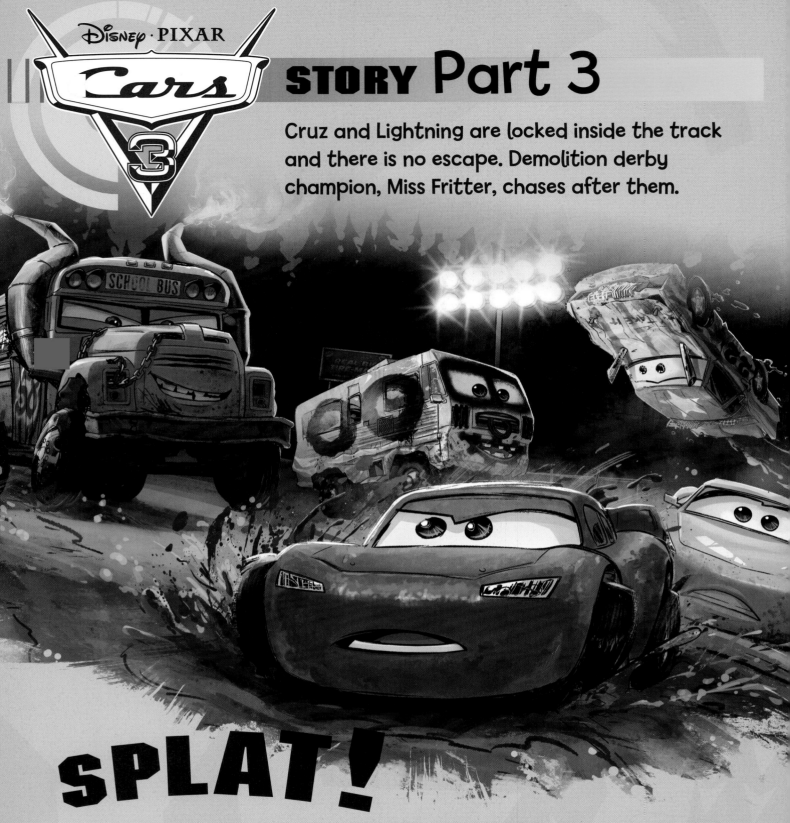

SPLAT!

Lightning manages to distract Miss Fritter while Cruz escapes. Cruz gets the hang of the muddy track and ends up winning the contest.

Cruz tells Lightning how much she loved winning the demolition derby. She has always wanted to race, but has never felt good enough.

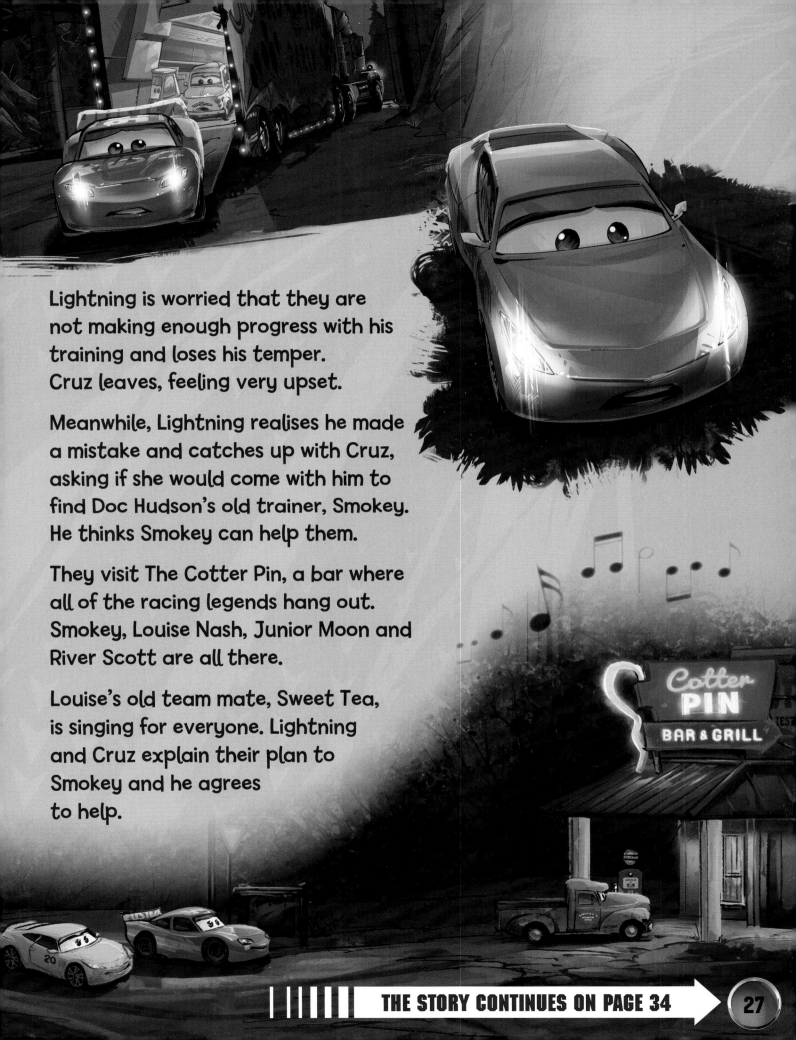

Lightning is worried that they are not making enough progress with his training and loses his temper. Cruz leaves, feeling very upset.

Meanwhile, Lightning realises he made a mistake and catches up with Cruz, asking if she would come with him to find Doc Hudson's old trainer, Smokey. He thinks Smokey can help them.

They visit The Cotter Pin, a bar where all of the racing legends hang out. Smokey, Louise Nash, Junior Moon and River Scott are all there.

Louise's old team mate, Sweet Tea, is singing for everyone. Lightning and Cruz explain their plan to Smokey and he agrees to help.

THE STORY CONTINUES ON PAGE 34

Miss Fritter's
FACT CHECK

WATCH OUT! Fierce Miss Fritter wants to test your *Cars 3* knowledge.

ANSWER as many of her questions as you can. You can do this in teams if you like, or just test yourself.

1 Who is from the Next Generation of racers?

A ☐ Junior "Midnight" Moon

B ☐ Jackson Storm

2

Who helps Lightning and Cruz get ready to race?

A ☐ Natalie Certain

B ☐ Smokey

3

Where does Sweet Tea sing?

A ☐ Wheel Well Hotel

B ☐ The Cotter Pin

4 What is the name of Lightning McQueen's new sponsor?

A ☐ Sterling

B ☐ Dollar

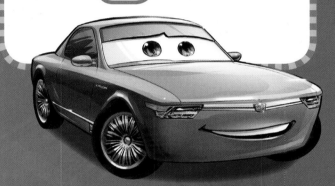

5

What number is Lightning McQueen?

A ☐ 24

B ☐ 95

Check your answers on page 68.

Natalie's NUMBERS

Natalie Certain knows her numbers!
PRACTISE your counting with Natalie and see if you can find everything she needs. **COLOUR** in the items as you find them.

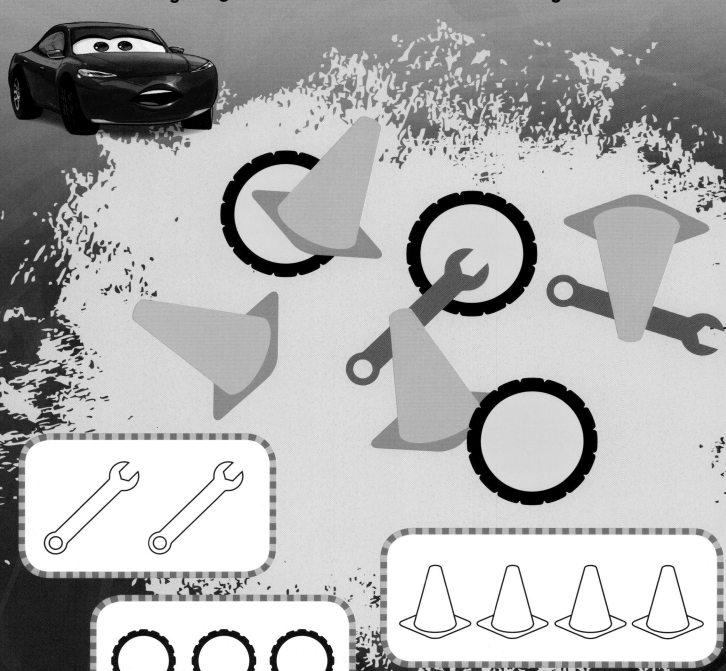

Check your answers on page 68.

DEMOLITION Derby

It's chaos at the demolition derby! Which racer will win? **WORK OUT** which track leads to the finish, to find out.

A

B

C

D

Check your answers on page 68.

Which Character are YOU?

Each *Cars* character has something special.
ANSWER the questions to find out who you're most like.

START HERE

PICK a colour

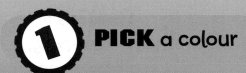

PICK your favourite

RED → ELEPHANT or CHEETAH?

BLUE → MAKING A DEN or PAINTING A PICTURE?

YELLOW → COMPUTER GAMES or PLAYING OUTDOORS?

CRUZ RAMIREZ

You are clever and funny and your friends know you will be a star!

MACK

Loyal and hardworking, you are a true friend.

GUIDO

Super helpful and a little bit cheeky, you love playing pranks.

MATER

No one has more fun than you. You are always there for your friends.

LIGHTNING MCQUEEN

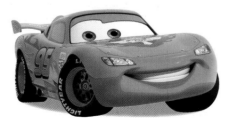

You are full of energy and enjoy having fun with your friends.

SALLY

You are smart and kind and always stick up for your friends.

33

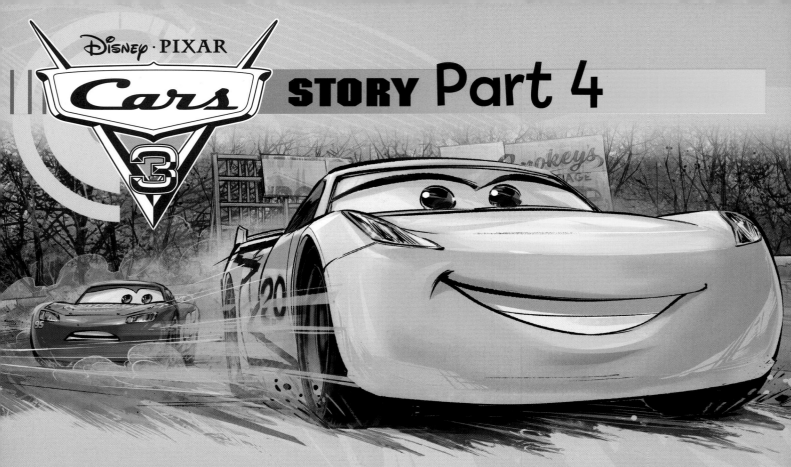

Smokey is tough on Lightning and makes him work very hard. They add racing tyres, a spoiler and other modifications to Cruz so she races, and looks, like Jackson Storm. They make Lightning train against her.

Cruz is fast, but has to learn about real racing. She starts to pick up tricks from Lightning and soon gets much better.

The season begins and Lightning races as fast as he can. As he gets closer to Jackson Storm, he realises Cruz deserves a chance to race.

Lightning pulls into the pit and tells Cruz to take his place. Ramone paints a #95 on Cruz and she's away.

Cruz quickly gets into second place, but Storm won't give up easily. He only cares about winning.

He blocks Cruz against the wall, but she flips across him and flies into first place. She has won! Cruz, Lightning and the team are thrilled.

Tex Dinoco offers a sponsorship deal to Cruz. She is going to be the Dinoco team's new star racer! She wears #51, Doc's number, to pay tribute to him.

Lightning appears in Doc's colours. He is Cruz's crew chief. Although he will continue to race, for now he can guide Cruz through her racing career, just like Doc did for him.

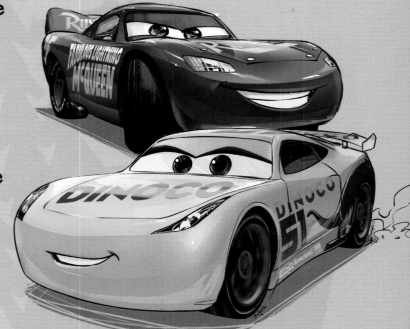

THE END

Sterling STARS

Cruz and Lightning both know that they'll need to work as a team to defeat Jackson Storm.

HELP
Lightning to find which shadow belongs to Cruz.

1

2

3

4

5

6

Check your answer on page 68.

© 2017 Disney/Pixar

CUT ALONG HERE

MATCHING
Pairs

Match the pairs of characters to make a set. You can draw lines or cut them out and play snap with a friend!

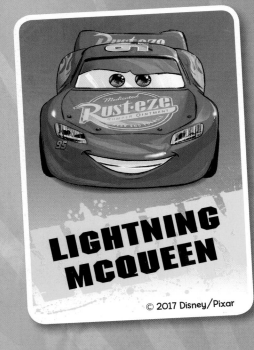

LIGHTNING MCQUEEN

© 2017 Disney/Pixar

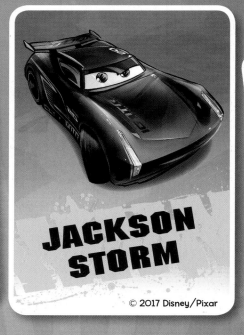

JACKSON STORM

© 2017 Disney/Pixar

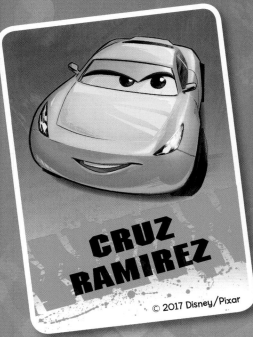

CRUZ RAMIREZ

© 2017 Disney/Pixar

DOC HUDSON

© 2017 Disney/Pixar; Hudson Hornet

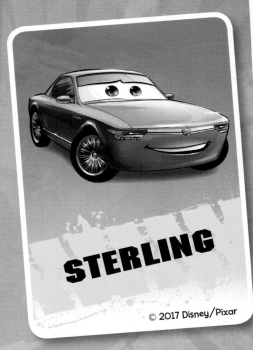

STERLING

© 2017 Disney/Pixar

MISS FRITTER

© 2017 Disney/Pixar

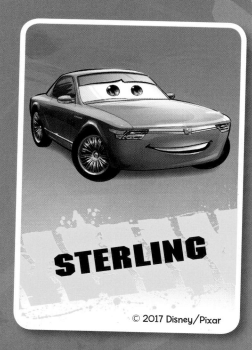

STERLING

© 2017 Disney/Pixar

JACKSON STORM

© 2017 Disney/Pixar

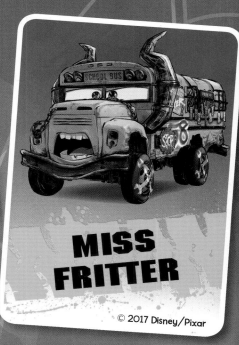

MISS FRITTER

© 2017 Disney/Pixar

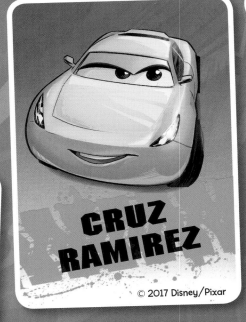

CRUZ RAMIREZ

© 2017 Disney/Pixar

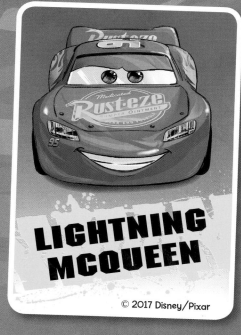

LIGHTNING MCQUEEN

© 2017 Disney/Pixar

Make sure you ask an adult to help you with cutting out.

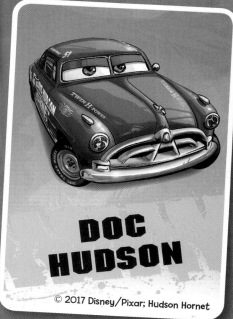

DOC HUDSON

© 2017 Disney/Pixar; Hudson Hornet

DREAM TEAM

© 2017 Disney/Pixar

JIGSAW
Jumble

Now that Sterling sponsors Lightning McQueen, the racer must ask for one more chance to show he is good enough to race.

1

2

3

4

5

Can you **SEE** which of the jigsaw pieces appear in the big picture?

Check your answers on page 68.

Training
MASTER

Help Lightning McQueen get to grips with the new racing technology. **COMPLETE** the page and he'll be race-ready!

F X THE GLITCH

The screens of the racing simulator have gone fuzzy. Which of the three screens shows Lightning's friend Cruz Ramirez?

1

2

3

AGLE EYE

Lightning is going to have to pay attention if he is to compete against the Next Gen racers. Can you do that too? **ANSWER** the questions about the picture.

1 Lightning is in the lead. True or false?

2 How many cars are in the race?

3 What colour is Lightning?

Check your answers on page 69.

Get DESIGNING

Every star racer needs to look the part. If you were a race car, what would you go for? **DRAW** your design below.

You could add go-faster stripes, polka dots, or anything else you like!

ZOOM In

Which of the close-ups can be found in the picture below?

COLOUR in the cup above each image which appears in the big picture.

1

2

3

4

5

Check your answers on page 69.

When Lightning McQueen ends up in Radiator Springs by mistake, he doesn't make a good first impression with the locals.

Unable to find his way back to the camera crews and celebrity of racing, Lightning has some lessons to learn about teamwork — and his new friends are very happy to help.

Best FRIENDS

Let's head back to Radiator Springs and visit Lightning McQueen's friends.

MATER

Mater is a lovable tow truck. His paint work is a little rusty but he's a loyal friend! He gets a kick out of tipping tractors and waking up Fred, the scary bulldozer.

SALLY

Sally gave up a fast-paced life in California to live in beautiful Radiator Springs. Sally is very smart and wants to put her beloved town "back on the map".

SHERIFF

Sheriff is a 1949 police cruiser who takes his role as peace-keeper very seriously. With a big moustache grill and squishy tyres, Sheriff loves to tell stories about the good old days.

RAMONE

Ramone runs Radiator Springs' custom paint shop. He is a great artist and loves to give friends makeovers.

FLO

Flo runs the V8 Café where she serves the "finest fuel in fifty states". No-nonsense Flo used to be a glamorous show car, but now prefers to rule the roost of Radiator Springs.

RAMONE'S
House of Body Art

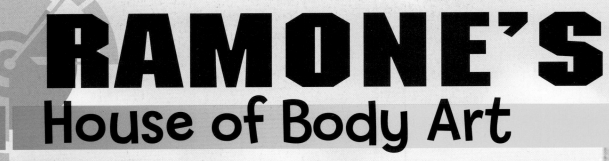

Lightning McQueen and his friends have visited Ramone's workshop to get spruced up.

TRACE the word under each character to find out which colour paint Ramone should use.

Lightning McQueen

red

Flo

green

48

COLOUR in the paint splodges to match each character.

Sally

Mater

blue

brown

Luigi

yellow

TRACTOR
Tipping

Which 2 tractors below make a **MATCHING** pair?

Lightning and Mater are tipping tractors.

3

2

1

6

5

4

Check your answer on page 69.

Team MCQUEEN

Lightning and Guido are getting ready to race.

COLOUR in the picture below.

Can you **COUNT** how many flags there are in the picture?

Check your answers on page 69.

Super STATIONERY

Make your own Lightning McQueen pen pot.

YOU WILL NEED:

☆ 1 empty juice carton ☆ Scissors ☆ Colouring pencils
☆ A4 piece of card ☆ Glue ☆ Red felt tip pen or red paper

ALWAYS ask for an adult's help when using scissors!

1 **ASK** an adult to cut the juice carton so it's about 10cm high. **COLOUR** it in red or cover it with red paper.

2 **CUT** out the template and stick it to the A4 piece of cardboard. **COLOUR** in Lightning McQueen using the coloured dots as a guide. Then **ASK** an adult to cut out both pieces.

3 **COLOUR** in the back of the cardboard cut-outs in red.

4 Now **GLUE** two sides of the carton and stick on your front and back templates. Once it's dried you can fill it with your favourite pencils!

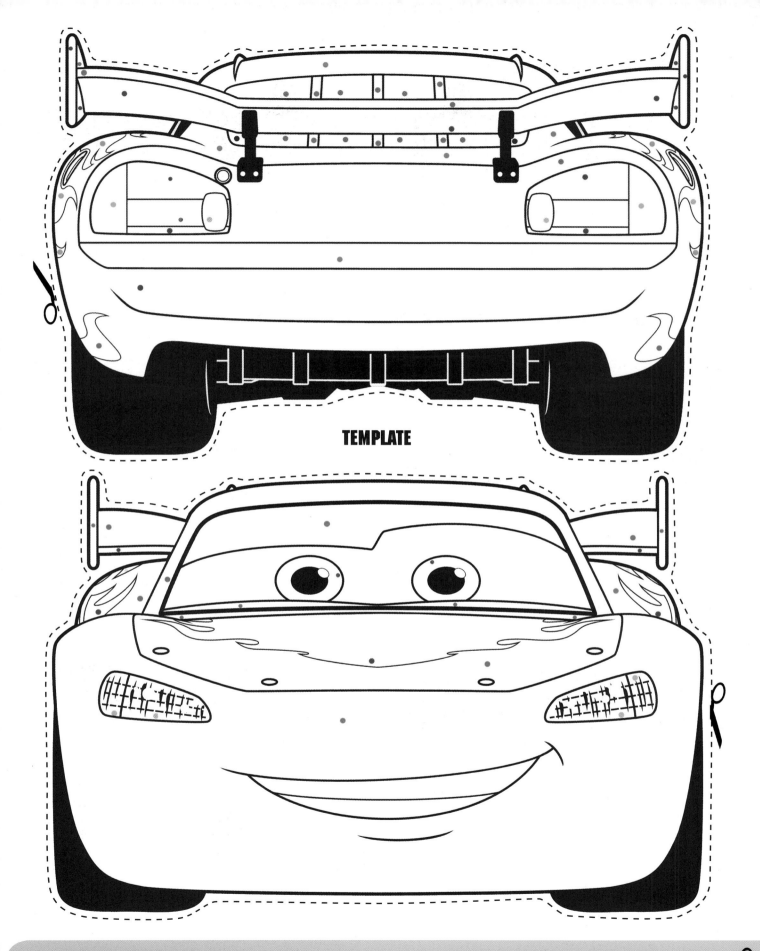

TEMPLATE

Don't forget to finish the puzzles on the next page before you cut anything out.

All Shapes and SIZES

Put the cars in order from smallest to largest.
WRITE the letters in the grid below.

A RED

B MACK

C LUIGI

D SALLY

E GUIDO

SMALLEST ⟶ **LARGEST**

Check your answers on page 69.

SEQUENCES

Which image comes next in each sequence?
DRAW your answer in the box.

1

2

3

4

Check your answers on page 69.

MAKE
a Best Friend Card

Mater is sending his best friend, Lightning McQueen, a postcard. Help him by colouring, sticking and gluing decorations that you think Lightning McQueen would like.

YOU WILL NEED:

☆ Scissors
(ask an adult to help when using these)

☆ Piece of card

☆ Glue

☆ Coloured pens

3 Colour in the picture using your best friend's favourite colours.

4 Use decorations to make the card extra special. There are some ideas below but you can use whatever you like! THREAD, WOOL, BUTTONS, GLITTER PENS, SEQUINS or OLD WRAPPING PAPER.

1 Cut out the next page and glue it to your piece of card.

2 Spread out some newspaper to protect the table or floor you are working on.

5 When it is dry, write your message inside and give it to your friend.

© 2017 Disney/Pixar

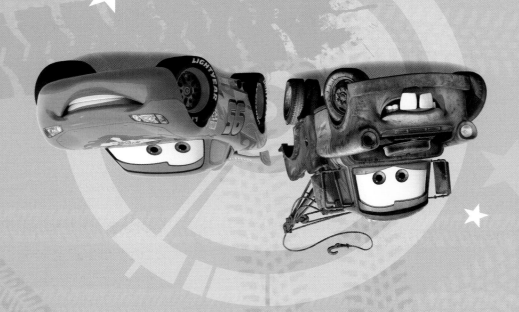

FOLD ALONG HERE

BEST FRIENDS

From ....

BEST FRIEND!

You are my

Dear ....

Pit Stop
PUZZLE

Sheriff, Mack and Sally want to get to Radiator Springs.
Follow the tracks to see which one makes it.

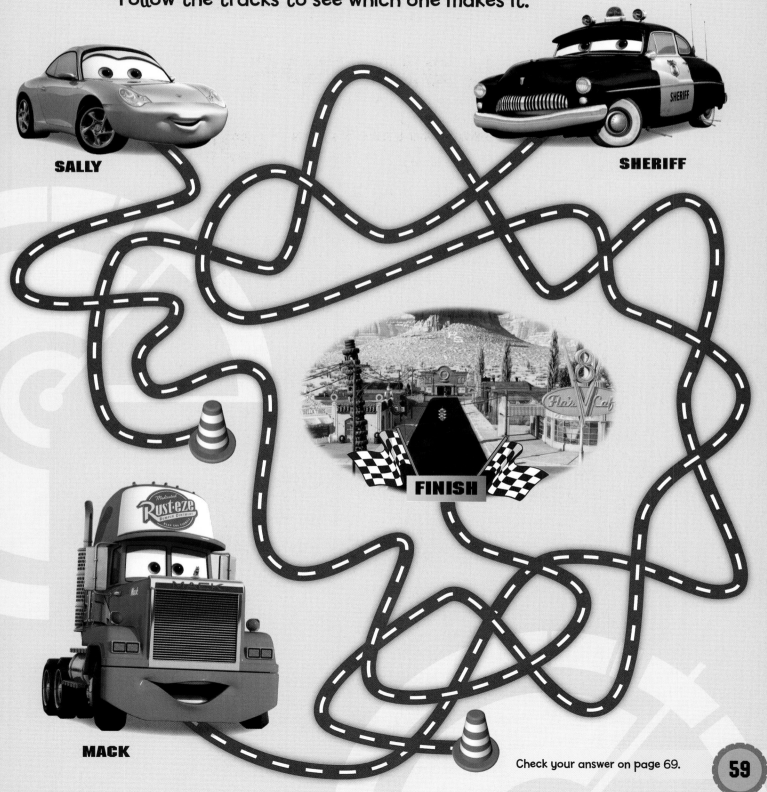

SALLY

SHERIFF

FINISH

MACK

Check your answer on page 69.

Memory
CHALLENGE

It's time to put your memory skills to the test.

To **TEST** your memory, cover the picture while you answer the questions.

STUDY the picture and then **ANSWER** true or false to the questions by colouring in the box next to your answer.

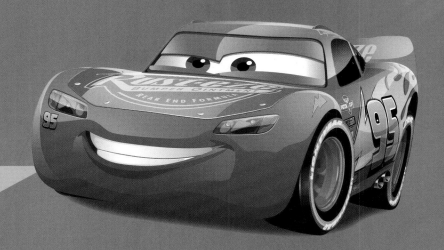

1 Lightning McQueen is not in this picture.

TRUE ☐

FALSE ☐

2 Mater is smiling.

TRUE ☐

FALSE ☐

3 There are 52 vehicles in the picture.

TRUE ☐

FALSE ☐

4 Guido has a wig on.

TRUE ☐

FALSE ☐

Check your answers on page 69.

Radiator
SPRINGS

YOU WILL NEED: Counters or Coins 1 x Dice

Lightning McQueen is visiting Radiator Springs. **PLAY** the game with a friend to see who wins!

START

1

2 You find a short cut. **RACE AHEAD TO SPACE 11**

14

13

12 Flo fills up your tank! **RACE AHEAD TO SPACE 17**

11

15 Mater fixes-up your engine! **ZOOM FORWARD 3 SPACES**

16 You take a wrong turn. **MOVE BACK TO SPACE 13**

17

18

Place your counters on **START** and roll the dice to move. If you land on a special space, follow the instructions!

3

4

5
Fillmore's organic fuel gives you extra speed.
MOVE FORWARD 1 SPACE

6

7
Lizzie has forgotten what she needs help with!
MISS A TURN

8

9
You owe a parking fine!
GO BACK TO SPACE 4

10

19
You decide to get some rest at the Cozy Cone Hotel!
MOVE BACK 1 SPACE

20

FINISH

SALLY'S
Odd One Out

Can you **FIND** which picture of Sally is the odd one out?
CIRCLE your answer.

1

2

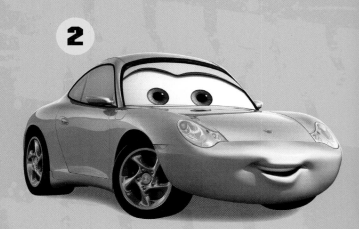

3

4

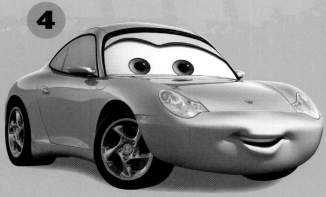

5

Check your answer on page 69.

Fearsome FRANK

Mater is tipping tractors again and has disturbed Frank the Bulldozer. Help him to escape before Frank charges.

GUIDE Mater through the maze. Avoid the obstacles and get back to the safety of the Junk Yard.

START

FINISH

Check your answer on page 69.

Painting
TRACKS

Why not **PAINT** your very own racetrack? Then you'll be able to race like your favourite *Cars* characters!

YOU WILL NEED:

☆ A large sheet of paper

☆ Old newspaper

☆ Bowls of different coloured paint

☆ Small toy cars
(You can use motorbikes, trucks or tractors too!)

Put down old newspapers to protect the floor or table you're working on. Set up your paint pots, cars and sheet of paper. Dip the wheels of your cars in a pot of paint — each car can use a different colour. Drive the cars all over your piece of paper and watch your amazing racing tracks appear!

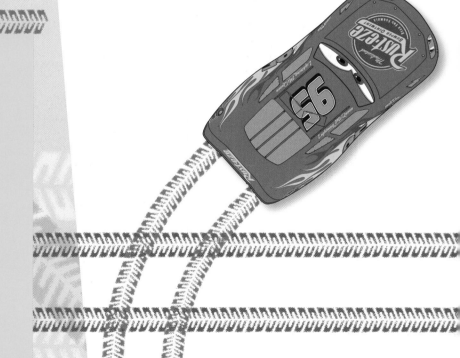

ANSWERS

PAGE 15 Storm Ahead

PAGE 16 Doc Hudson

PAGE 20 Next Generation

PAGE 21 Where is Everybody?
A, B, C, E and F are in the picture.
D — Storm Jackson isn't.

PAGE 24 Who is Who?
1 -D, 2 - E, 3 - B, 4 - A, 5 - C.

PAGE 28 Miss Fritter's Fact Check
1 -B, 2 - B, 3 - B, 4 - A, 5 - B.

PAGE 30 Natalie's Numbers
2 spanners

3 wheels

4 traffic cones

PAGE 31 Demolition Derby
C - Cruz is set to win the race.

PAGE 36 Sterling Stars
Shadow shape 6 is Cruz.

PAGE 41 Jigsaw Jumble
Pieces 2 and 3 fit the picture.

PAGE 42 Training Master
FIX THE GLITCH
Picture 2 is Cruz.

EAGLE EYE
1 – False. Cruz is winning.
2 – 3 cars are in the race.
3 – Lightning is red.

PAGE 44 Zoom In
Close-ups 1, 4 and 5 are
in the picture.

PAGE 50 Tractor Tipping
2 and 4 are a matching pair.

PAGE 51 Team McQueen

There are 6 flags.

PAGE 54 All Shapes and sizes

E C D A B
SMALLEST ⟶ LARGEST

PAGE 55 Sequences

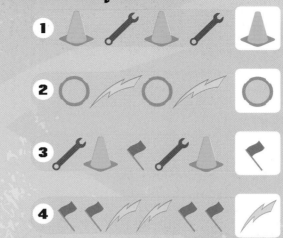

PAGE 59 Pit Stop Puzzle
Sally is going to Radiator Springs.

PAGE 60 Memory Challenge
1 – False
2 – True
3 – False. There are 11 vehicles.
4. True

PAGE 64 Sally's Odd One Out
Picture 3 is odd one out.

PAGE 65 Fearsome Frank

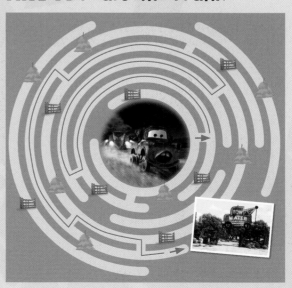